# The
# Magic Bag Ositos

Story by P A Davie
Illustrations by B A Lee

For Mum and Dad.


With thanks to Nick Buchanan

First Published 2012 by Appin Press, an imprint of Countyvise Ltd
14 Appin Road, Birkenhead, CH41 9HH.

Second edition 2018

British Library Cataloguing in Publication Data.
A catalogue record for this book is available from the British Library.

ISBN 978 1721719525

In a hidden away corner of an overgrown, evergreen *jardín* (khar-deen) something is stirring in the early *mañana.* (man-yan-a)

Can you hear someone singing? It's coming from that bag. *Escucha.* (ess-koot-cha) Listen...

"*Somos somos ositos* (so-mose oz-ee-toes)

We are teddy bears

*Somos somos ositos*

We are teddy bears

*Somos somos ositos*

We are teddy bears

*Somos somos ositos*

We are teddy bears, hey!"


Who is it in the bag?

*¿Quién está, en la bolsa?* (key-en ess-ta en la bol-sa)

*¿Quién está, en la bolsa?*

*¿Quién está, en la bolsa?*

Who is in the bag?


*¿Quién está, en la bolsa?*

*¿Quién está, en la bolsa?*

*¿Quién está, en la bolsa?*

Who is in the bag?

4

It's someone who can *hablar español* (ab-lar ess-pan-yol) - speak Spanish.

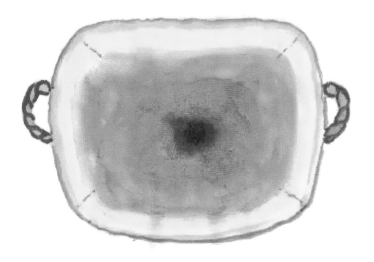

## (CHANT!)

**(To the tune of: Frère Jacques):**

*Habla (ab-la) español,*

*Habla español,*

Speak speak Spanish,

Speak speak Spanish,

*Habla español,*

*Habla español,*

Speak speak Spanish,

Speak speak Spanish.

Oh! It's the Magic Bag *Ositos!* They're teddy bears that live in the magic bag and, at the bottom of this *bolsa mágica (bol-sa mak-ee-kha)*, there is a magic cave! They've just woken up.

Let's see what they are doing....

**(CHANT!)**

*¡Mira por favor!* (mee-ra por fa-boor)

*¡Mira por favor!*

Look! Look! Please!

Look! Look! Please!

*¡Mira por favor!*

*¡Mira por favor!*

Look! Look! Please!

Look! Look! Please!

One of the Magic Bag *Ositos* is on the bouncy castle.

They bounce, bounce, b-o-u-n-c-e on the bouncy *castillo* *(cast-eel-yo)*, you see, and leap out of the magic bag, so stand back. Can you guess who it is? Go on, *adivina* *(ad-ee-bee-na)*. Guess. Who is it? Will it be Granville or Moucheboeuf? Or will it be Jolie Holly or Trixie?

**(To the tune of: Baa Baa Black Sheep):**

*A-di-vi-na,*

*Adivina quien es,*

*¿Quién es? ¿Quién es?*

Guess who it is?

*A-di-vi-na,*

*Adivina quien es,*

*¿Quién es? ¿Quién es?*

Guess who it is?

"Wheeeeeeeeeeeeeee!
*¡Soy yo! (soy yoe)* It's me!"

It's Granville! Let's say hello. *¡Hola
(o-la)* Granville! He's fetching in the milk.

Oh, watch out! Here comes
Moucheboeuf, too.

"Wheeeeeeeeeeeeeee!"

*¡Hola* Moucheboeuf!

They both say to each other: "*¡Es mi amigo!* *(ess mee am-ee-go)*
He's my friend!"

Granville is now asking Moucheboeuf how he is.

**(CHANT!)**

"*¿Cómo estás? ¿Cómo estás? ¿Cómo estás?* (ko-mo ess-tass)

How are you?

*¿Cómo estás? ¿Cómo estás? ¿Cómo estás?*

How are you?"


Moucheboeuf replies,

**(CHANT!)**

"*Muy bien gracias, muy bien gracias,*

*Muy bien gracias,* (mwee bee-en gra-thee-ass)

Very well, thank you.

*Muy bien gracias, muy bien gracias, muy bien gracias,*

Very well, thank you.


*¿Y qué tal?* (ee kay tal)
And how are you? How's things?"

"Great", says Granville,
holding up his two thumbs.

"¡*Fenomenal!¡Fenomenal!* *(fen-om-en-al)* Come on, Moucheboeuf, let's go back down to the magic *cueva* *(kway-ba)* and have some breakfast. I think we've woken up Jolie Holly and Trixie. I'll get the milk."

Granville's *sombrero* *(som-brer-o)* falls off his head as he bends down to fetch *las botellas de leche* *(lass bot-ell-yas day letch-ay)*.

"Oh, I'll pick your hat up Granville", says Moucheboeuf helpfully.

Granville replies: "Thanks Moucheboeuf. Can you put it on my toe?"

"Put it on your toe?", exclaims Moucheboeuf. "On your *dedo del pie?* *(day-do del pee-ay)* Granville –

**(To the tune of: She'll be coming round the mountain):**

You don't wear your *sombrero* on your toe,

You don't wear your *sombrero* on your toe,

You don't wear your *sombrero,*

Don't wear your *sombrero,*

You don't wear your *sombrero* on your toe.

Your *sombrero* goes on your *cabeza,* *(cab-ay-tha)*
Granville! Not on your *dedo del pie!*"

"Well put it on my cabbage then", requests his friend.

"I said on your *cabeza*", repeats Moucheboeuf "your head,
not your cabbage!"

Granville and Moucheboeuf jump back into the magic bag and are met by
the two girls.

*Las chicas* (lass cheek-ass) greet them by saying: "¡*Buenos días*
Granville! ¡*Buenos días* Moucheboeuf!" (bway-noss dee-ass)

"Good morning to you as well Trixie! Hi Jolie Holly! Are you both *bien?*" *(bee-en)*, asks Granville.

"*No.* *(no)* We're not fine, I'm *no muy bien* *(mwee bee-en)*, I'm not very good, because I banged my *boca* *(bo-ka)*."

13

"Ooh my *boca!*", Trixie moans as she touches her mouth. "Ooh *me duele la boca! (may dway-lay la bo-ka)* My mouth hurts! I bumped into Jolie Holly on the bouncy *castillo* and fell off."

"Ooh my *espalda!*" *(esp-al-da)*, whines Jolie Holly, clutching her back. "Ooh my *cuello (kwell-yoe)* and ooh my *cabeza, tengo dolor de cabeza*", *(ten-go dol-or day cab-ay-tha)* she continues, rubbing her neck and then the top of her head.

"My headache is getting better though so now I'm, *regular (regg-oo-lar)*, just so-so."

"Ooh, *tengo hambre*" *(am-bray)*, says Moucheboeuf.

"I'm hungry too", Granville adds. "Maybe the thought of *desayuno (dess-aye-oo-no)* will make you two girls feel *bien.*"

Jolie Holly and Trixie sing: "What's for *desayuno,* what's for *desayuno,* what's for breakfast?"

"*Pan*" *(pan)*, says Granville.

"Pants!", exclaims Jolie Holly. "Did you say pants? You can't eat your pants for breakfast!"

"I said *pan,* not pants! *¡Pan!* Bread!"

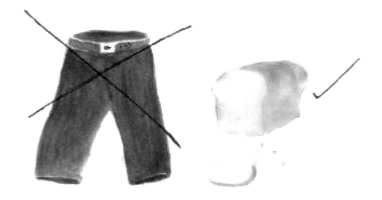

Granville and Moucheboeuf sing:

**(To the tune of: This Old Man):**
"*Pan pan pan, pan pan pan, pan pan pan pan pan pan pan, pan pan pan pan pan* and jam, *pan pan pan pan pan* and jam.*"

"Ooh, *mi preferido*" *(mee pref-er-ee-doe)*, says Trixie "bread and *mermelada.*" *(mer-mel-ad-da)*

The girls, Jolie Holly and Trixie lay *la mesa (may-sa)*, whilst *los chicos (loss cheek-oss)*, Moucheboeuf and Granville prepare the bread and jam for breakfast. They also make *té (tay)* and *café. (kaff-ay)*

"*¿Té o (o) café,* Granville?", asks Jolie Holly.

"Tea, *por favor.*"

"Moucheboeuf?", Jolie Holly calls.

"Coffee, please."

Both of the boys shout, "*¡Muchas gracias!* (moo-chass grath-ee-ass) Thank you very much!"

Just then the phone rings.

"*¡Diga!* (dee-ga) Hello!" says Granville.

"*¿Quién es?* Who is it? *¿Quién?* Oh Mooey! Mooey *Vaca!* (bak-a) *¡Hola! ¿Qué tal?*"

(It's Mooey Vaca, a friend of the *ositos,* on the phone.)

"*Muy bien*", replies Mooey Vaca.

"*¿Qué pasa* Mooey? (pa-sa) What's going on? *¿Qué?* What?", says Granville "it's your birthday?

**(To the tune of: He's a Jolly Good Fellow):**

*¿Cuántos años tienes?* *(Kwan-towse ann-yose tee-en-ace)*

*¿Cuántos años tienes? ¿Cuántos años tienes?*

How old are you?


How old are you? How old are you?

*¿Cuántos años tienes? ¿Cuántos años tienes?*

*¿Cuántos años tienes?* How old are you?"


Mooey Vaca replies,


**(To the tune of: The Hokey Cokey):**

"*Tengo cinco (theen-ko) años,*

*Tengo cinco años,*

*Tengo cinco años,*

I am 5 years old, old, old."


**1**      **2**      **3**      **4**      **5**

*Uno (oo-no)*   *dos (doss)*   *tres (trayce)*   *cuatro (kwa-tro)*   *cinco (theen-koe)*


"Moucheboeuf!", Granville calls, "It's Mooey Vaca's *cumpleaños* *(kump-lee-ann-yose)*. She's 5 years old and she's invited us to her party today. Can we go?"


"I didn't know she was having *una fiesta (oo-na fee-es-ta)* -

**(CHANT!)**

*¡Hoy, hoy, hoy!* *(oy)* Today, today, today!

*¡Hoy, hoy, hoy!* Today, today, today!

*¡Hoy, hoy, hoy!* Today, today, today!

*¡Hoy, hoy, hoy!* Today, today, today!",

says Moucheboeuf in surprise. "What day is it *hoy?* Is it? -

**(To the tune of: Ring-A-Ring-A-Roses):**

*lunes* *(loon-ace)*, *martes* *(mart-ace)*, *miércoles* *(mee-erk-ol-ace)*,

*jueves* *(kweb-ace)*, *viernes* *(be-er-nace)*,

*sábado* *(sab-a-doe)*, *o domingo* *(dom-een-goe)* - the days of the week.

*lunes, martes, miércoles,*

*jueves, viernes,*

*sábado o domingo* - the days of the week.

Monday, Tuesday, Wednesday, Thursday, Friday, Saturday

Or Sunday, Sunday - the days of the week."

"It's *martes*", answers Granville.

"We can go then", confirms Moucheboeuf. "We're not doing anything special today. Ask her where she lives, Granville, because she's just moved house."

"*¡Vale!* *(bal-ay)* OK!", says Granville. "Mooey,

18

*¿Dónde vives, dónde vives?* *(don-day bee-base)* Where do you live?

*¿Dónde vives, dónde vives?* Where do you live?

*¿Dónde vives, dónde vives?* Where do you live?

*¿Dónde vives, dónde vives?* Where do you live?"

"¡*Vivo (bee-bo), v-i-v-ooooooooooo en* Liverpool!", shouts Mooey Vaca.

**(To the tune of: He's a Jolly Good Fellow):**

"*Vivo en* Liverpool, *vivo en* Liverpool,

I live in Liverpool, I live in Liverpool, I live in Liverpool,

*vivo en* Liverpool."

"We know you live in Liverpool, but what street? *¿Qué calle?*
*(kal-yay)*... *¿Calle* Moo? *¿Calle* Moo?", asks Granville.

"Yes, *calle* Moo. It's by the *Zoo (thoo)* streets," Mooey explains.

**(CHANT!)**

"*No entiendo, no entiendo* *(no ent-ee-en-doe)*

I don't understand,

*No entiendo, no entiendo*

I don't understand,

*No entiendo, no entiendo*

I don't understand,

19

*No entiendo, no entiendo*
I don't understand", adds Granville puzzled.

"Ah, *yo entiendo*", says Trixie. "All the streets around where she lives are called the Zoo streets. They are named after *animales*." *(an-ee-mal-ace)*

"*¿Zoo (thoo)* streets, *zoo (thoo)* streets?", asks Moucheboeuf perplexed. "Like *zorro (tho-roe)* street or *cebra (theb-ra)* street? I'm thorry but I've never heard of a fox or zebra street. Really thorry."

"There's no fox or zebra street but there is a *calle* Gnu", confirms Trixie.

"*¿Calle* Gnu, *calle* Gnu?", exclaim Granville and Moucheboeuf.

"*Calle* Gnu is next to *calle* Shrew."

"*¿Calle* Shrew, *calle* Shrew?"

"And *calle* Shrew is across from *calle* Cockatoo."

"Cockatoo, Cockatoo?"

"And *calle* Cockatoo is by *calle* Emu."

"Emu too, Emu too?"

"Which is near to *calle* Roo."

"*¿Calle* Roo, *calle* Roo?"

"Roo is short for kangaroo", explains Jolie Holly, "*¿entiendes (ent-ee-end-ace)* Moucheboeuf, *tú (too)* entiendes Granville? Do you understand?"

"Hold on, let me get this right," says a confused Granville.

"*Calle* Roo is by *calle* Zoo, so, *calle* Gnu and *calle* Shrew are Kangaroos, and Emus are Cockatoos. And then there's *calle* Moo, which is short for *calle* Kangamoo."

"No!!!", cries an exasperated Trixie. "*Calle* Moo is by the Zoo streets, so, *calle* Gnu and *calle* Shrew, are Zoo streets, and so are *calle* Cockatoo and *calle* Emu, too. And then there's *calle* Roo, which is short for *calle* Kangaroo!"

"Oh! Poo! I wish I'd never asked about *calle* Moo!," complains Granville.

"What's the number of your *casa (ca-sa)* Mooey?", enquires Granville. "*¿Veinte? (bayn-tay) De acuerdo (day-ak-wer-do)*, Mooey. We'll see you later."

They all shout, "*¡Hasta luego!*" *(ass-ta loo-ay-go)*

Mooey answers: "See you later as well!"

The Magic Bag *Ositos* have breakfast. As soon as they've finished Granville says, "Right everybody let's get ready for the *fiesta.* Let's get washed. Moucheboeuf, you go in the bath and I'll go in the *ducha. (doo-cha)* Then Jolie Holly and Trixie can get ready."

21

Moucheboeuf gets ready for his *baño* (ban-yo) and Granville gets
in the shower. They both sing whilst washing.

**(To the tune of: Here We Go Round The Mulberry Bush):**

"*Así es como me lavo las manos* (ah-see ess koe-mo may  la-bo lass man-oss)
*Me lavo las manos, me lavo las manos,*
*Así es como me lavo las manos,*
*Me lavo las manos.*
This is how I wash my hands,
Wash my hands, wash my hands,
This is how I wash my hands,
Wash my hands."

Then they wash their hair.

"*Así es como me lavo el pelo* (pel-o)
*Me lavo el pelo, me lavo el pelo,*
*Así es como me lavo el pelo,*
*Me lavo el pelo.*
This is how I wash my hair,
Wash my hair, wash my hair,
This is how I wash my hair,
Wash my hair."

"Hey, there's a cockroach flying around in here!", shouts Moucheboeuf.

*La cucaracha (kook-a-rat-cha)* flies into *la ducha.* Granville screams in fright and chases the flying cockroach around trying to shoo it away.

"*¡Ven aquí! (ben ak-ee)* Come here!

**(To the tune of: Mexican Folk Song - La Cucaracha)**
*La cucaracha, la cucaracha, ven ven ven aquí,*
*La cucaracha, la cucaracha, ven ven ven aquí,*
*La cucaracha, la cucaracha, ven ven ven aquí,*
*La cucaracha, la cucaracha, ven ven ven aquí.*"

The *cucaracha* manages to escape but then returns to *la ducha* just as Granville is opening his *boca* to sing again. The *cucaracha en la ducha* then flies straight into his mouth. Gulp! He's swallowed the cockroach.

"I've just swallowed that *cucaracha!*", he gasps.

Meanwhile, in the bedroom Jolie Holly and Trixie are deciding what clothes to wear for *la fiesta.* "I think I'll wear these *vestidos (best-ee-dos)* - this pink skirt and purple *blusa (bloo-sa),*" Jolie Holly decides.

"Yes", agrees Trixie, "*rosa (ro-sa)* and *morado (mor-ad-o)* go together. *Mi (mee) tía (tee-a),* Auntie Rosa with the pink face always wears purple. I'm going to wear *una falda (fal-da)* and a blouse as well. How about this yellow *falda?*"

"That's a lovely skirt and *amarillo (ama-reel-yo)* is my favourite *color*" *(kol-or),* adds Jolie Holly. "That's a nice red party dress you have as well, Trixie.

My Auntie, Tía María with the red face always wears *rojo (rok-ho)* but my *tío (tee-o)*, Tío Custard, he likes *azul.*" *(ath-ool)*

"Tío Custard? Tío Custard is like a fool?", questions Trixie.

"No!" says Jolie Holly. "I said Tío Custard likes *azul* - blue. He's not a fool. He's not *un tonto (ton-toe)*, but he is a little bit crazy, *un poco loco (oon poe-koe loe-koe)*, just like Tío Mustard."

"Tío Mustard? Tío Custard and Tío Mustard? Uncle Custard and Uncle Mustard? They're funny names!", laughs Trixie.

"Now, I wore this *rojo* dress for my birthday *fiesta.* Mmm I can't make up my mind what to *llevar (lyay-bar)* – the red *vestido (best-ee-doe)* or the yellow *falda.*"

"Wear the *rojo* party dress again. It's *fantástico!*" *(fan-tast-ee-koe)*, Jolie Holly tells her friend.

Trixie decides to wear the red dress.

"The *cuarto de baño* (kwar-toe-day-ban-yo) is free girls!", calls Moucheboeuf.

"OK, *de acuerdo*", reply *las chicas.*

So, the girls enter the bathroom to get washed and the *chicos* go into their bedroom to get dressed.

"I'm going to wear my white *pantalón* (pan-ta-lon) and a *jersey azul*" (kher-say ), decides Moucheboeuf.

"Why don't you wear the same *colores* (kol-or-ace) as *yo,* Granville?"

"I can't", sighs Granville, "my *blanco (blan-koe)* trousers are dirty and my blue jumper has a hole in it. I'll wear this green *camisa (kam-ee-sa)*. Now which tie do you think goes with a shirt coloured *verde? (ber-day)* A brown one?"

"*No.* Not *marrón.*" *(mar-ron)*

"Black?"

"No. Not *negro. (negg-roe)* How about *gris? (greess)*", asks Moucheboeuf. "It's the one that you want, ooh, ooh, ooh hoo, it's the one that you want, ooh, ooh, ooh hoo."

"No! Grey is not the one that I want!" , shrieks Granville.

"What colour then?", enquires Moucheboeuf.

Granville sings

"*Rojo o amarillo,*

*Rojo o amarillo,*

*Naranja (na-ran-kha), azul, verde,*

*Naranja, azul, verde,*

*Gris, marrón, morado,*

*Gris, marrón, morado,*

*Negro, blanco, rosa,*

*Negro, blanco, rosa.*

Red or yellow,

Red or yellow,

Orange, blue, green,

Orange, blue, green,

Grey, brown or purple,

Grey, brown or purple,

Black, white, pink.

Black, white, pink."

"*Prefiero (pref-ee-er-ro)* the orange *corbata (kor-ba-ta)*", states Moucheboeuf.

"*Estoy (esst-oy) de acuerdo, naranja*", agrees Granville. "I'll wear my grey trousers as well."

Then Moucheboeuf starts to put on his *pantalón* as well. He sings:

**(To the tune of: Oh My Darling Clementine)**

"Oh *me pongo (may pon-go)*, oh *me pongo,*

Oh *me pongo el pantalón,*

Oh *me pongo,* oh *me pongo,* oh *me pongo el pantalón.*"

"Moucheboeuf", enquires Granville, "did you say 'pongy *pantalón?*' That means stinky pants!"

"No, I said '*me pongo el pantalón.*' That means 'I put on my trousers'. They're not pongy stinky pants! They're nice clean pants. Now I'm going to put my nice clean *calcetines (kal-the-teen-ace)* on my feet."

He sings again: **(To the tune of: Oh My Darling Clementine)**

"Oh *me pongo,* oh *me pongo,*

Oh *me pongo los calcetines,*

Oh *me pongo,* oh *me pongo,* oh *me pongo los calcetines.*"

"Hold it", Granville interrupts, "did you just say 'pongy *calcetines?*' Smelly socks!"

"No!", screeches Moucheboeuf, "I said '*me pongo los calcetines.*' I put on my socks. Nice clean socks. Not pongy smelly socks!"

The *ositos* are ready to leave.

"We'll get a card and a *regalo (re-gal-oe)* on the way to *la fiesta*", Jolie Holly pronounces. "Come on, everyone get on the bouncy *castillo.*"

The Magic Bag *Ositos* all get on the bouncy castle and start to BOUNCE, BOUNCE, B-O-U-N-C-E!!

"Hurrah!", they all scream and they bounce straight out of the magic bag.

# "Wheeeeeeeeeeeeeeee!"

They walk along the *camino* *(kam-een-o)* singing:

**(To the tune of: London Bridge is Falling Down)**

"*¡Vámonos!* *(bam-on-noss)* Let's go, let's go
Let's go, let's go
Let's go, let's go.
*¡Vámonos!* Let's go, let's go,
Let's go to the party.
*¡Vámonos!* Let's go, let's go
Let's go, let's go
Let's go, let's go.
*¡Vámonos!* Let's go, let's go,
Let's go to the party."

30

The Magic Bag *Ositos* go into *una tienda* (tee-en-da) to buy a present and a card. Trixie and Jolie Holly are going to select the card and Moucheboeuf and Granville are going to choose the *regalo.*

"Shall we buy a *juguete* (koo-get-tay) or a game or *un libro?* (lee-bro)", Granville asks Moucheboeuf but, Moucheboeuf is not there, he is over the other side of the shop playing with the toys.

Granville beckons his friend to come over. "Moucheboeuf! *¡Ven aquí!*

**(To the tune of: Head, Shoulders, Knees and Toes)**

*Ven aquí, ven acá, ven acá,* (ak-ka)

*Ven aquí, ven acá, ven acá,*

*Ven aquí, ven acá,*

*Ven aquí, ven acá, ven acá.*

We haven't got much time!"

But Moucheboeuf is in a world of his own playing with all the *juguetes* (koo-get-tays) and singing:

**(To the tune of: If Your Happy And You Know It Clap Your Hands)**

"If you want to *jugar* (khoo-gar) with *juguetes* (koo-get-tays) clap your hands,

If you want to *jugar* with *juguetes* clap your hands,

If you want to *jugar* with *juguetes*

*Jugar, jugar* with *juguetes*

*Jugar, jugar* with *juguetes*

Clap your hands."

"Moucheboeuf!", growls Granville angrily.
"*¡Ven acá!* Come over here!

**(CHANT!)**

*¡Date prisa! ¡Date prisa!* *(dat-ay pree-sa)*
Hurry up! Hurry up!
*¡Date prisa! ¡Date prisa!*
Hurry up! Hurry up!

**(CHANT!)**

*Ahora, ahora, ahora,* *(ah-ora)*
Now, now, now!
*Ahora, ahora, ahora,*
Now, now, now!"

"*¡Ya voy!* *(ya boy)* I'm coming!", calls Moucheboeuf. Moucheboeuf goes over and asks his friend why he is *enfadado* *(en-fad-ad-doe)*. Ooh *enfadado!* "Why are you so cross Granville?"

"*Estoy enfadado.* Ooh *enfadado!*", bellows Granville, "I am cross, because you are picking up all those toys and messing up the display. Also remember, you don't just touch anything in a shop because if it breaks you have to pay for it! Besides, you, are supposed to be helping me, choose a *regalo.* Now, I'll ask you again, shall we buy a toy or *un juego* *(kway-goe)* or a book?"

Moucheboeuf thinks. "*(Yo) pienso* *(yo pee-en-so)* — *un juego.*"

"I think a game also", Granville agrees.

The two *ositos* decide on a *regalo* and ask for it to be gift-wrapped.
Meanwhile Trixie and Jolie Holly have chosen *una tarjeta.* *(tar-khay-ta)*

"Give me some *dinero* *(dee-ner-o)* please Moucheboeuf", urges Granville.

Moucheboeuf starts chanting:
"Dinner dinner dinner dinner dinner dinner dinner - *¡dinero!*
Dinner dinner dinner dinner dinner dinner dinner - *¡dinero!*"

He then pulls something out of his pocket and drops it into Granville's
outstretched *mano.* *(ma-no)*

"Eeh! Yuk! What's that Moucheboeuf? Eeh! A soggy cheese and ham *bocadillo (bo-ka-deel-yo)* No, Moucheboeuf, that's your sandwich – your dinner from yesterday! I said give me some *dinero* - money - not your dinner!..Eeeeh!"

Moucheboeuf holds up the gift-wrapped present after Granville had payed for it (not with a soggy *queso (kes-so)* and *jamón (kham-on)* baguette but with proper *dinero*) and sings to the girls:

**(To the tune of: The Wheels On The Bus)**
"*Tengo un regalo,*
*¿Qué, qué es? ¿Qué, qué es? ¿Qué, qué es?*
*Tengo un regalo,*
*¿Qué, qué es?* What is it?
I've got a present,
What is it? What is it? What is it?
I've got a present,
*¿Qué, qué es?* What is it?"

"*¿Qué es?*", adds Granville.

"It's a *muñeca*" *(moon-yay-ka)*, guesses Jolie Holly.

"*No,* not a doll", says Moucheboeuf.

"A toy", adds Trixie.

"*No,* it's not a *juguete*", Granville states.

Jolie Holly says,

"*No sé, no sé, no lo sé (no loe say )*
*No sé, no sé, no lo sé*
*No sé, no sé, no lo sé*
I don't, I don't, I don't know!"

"*¡Yo lo sé!*" *(yo loe say),* exclaims Trixie, "It's a *juego.* A game."

"*Eso sí que es*" *(es-so see kay ess),* asserts Moucheboeuf.

"S-o-c-k-s?", Trixie spells. "Socks! I thought you said it was a *juego.*"

"It is a *juego!*", responds Moucheboeuf.

"But you've just spelt out the word s-o-c-k-s - socks, *verdad, verdad (ber-da), no?*", replies Trixie.

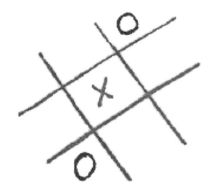

"No, I said, *eso sí que es.* It means 'yes, that's what it is'. *Eso sí que es* – a game called Tic-tac-toe", he explains.

"Tic, tac, toe?", they all exclaim, "that's a silly name for a *juego!*"

"*¿Vamos? (bam-oss)* Are we going?", urges Moucheboeuf, "the *autobús (ow-to-booss)* will be here soon."

"*Sí (see), sí, sí ¡vamos!* Yes, let's go!", everyone cries.

"*¡Vámonos!*
Let's go, let's go, let's go, let's go
Let's go, let's go,
*¡Vámonos!*
Let's go, let's go, let's go on the bus.
*¡Vámonos!*
Let's go, let's go, let's go, let's go
Let's go, let's go,
*¡Vámonos!*
Let's go, let's go, let's go on the bus."

The Magic Bag *Ositos* catch the *autobús* and get off near *calle* Moo.

"Here's *calle* Gnu and *calle* Emu", says Jolie Holly.

"*Aquí está (ak-ee es-ta) calle* Cockatoo", adds Trixie as they walk along.

"That's *calle* Shrew, *allá*" *(al-ya),* says Moucheboeuf pointing over the road. "And *calle* Poo is *allí.*" *(al-yee)*

"*¡Calle* Poo! *¡Calle* Poo!", they all exclaim.

**(CHANT!)**
"*¿Dónde, dónde está? ¿Dónde, dónde está? ¿Dónde, dónde está?*
Where is it?
*¿Dónde, dónde está? ¿Dónde, dónde está? ¿Dónde, dónde está?*
Where is it?"

"*Allí*....There....", Moucheboeuf indicates.

"No, that's *calle* **Roo**, not *calle* Poo!", laughs Jolie Holly.

The Magic Bag *Ositos* bounce up and down like kangaroos.

"*Aquí está* - Moo street!," shouts Trixie. "Let's find number *veinte.* Count everybody!"

| 1 | 2 | 3 | 4 | 5 | 6 | 7 | 8 | 9 | 10 | ! |
|---|---|---|---|---|---|---|---|---|---|---|
| *Uno* | *dos* | *tres* | *cuatro* | *cinco* | *seis* | *siete* | *ocho* | *nueve* | *¡diez!* | |
| (oo-no) | (doss) | (trayce) | (kwa-tro) | (theen-co) | (sayss) | (see-et-ay) | (o-cho) | (nu-eb-ay) | (dee-eth) | |

"It's that one, *allá,* over there, *número (nu-mer-o)* 10", cries Moucheboeuf!

"No, it's not, it's that one - *allí,* there, number 20. *Veinte* is 20. You can't count Moucheboeuf", laughs Trixie, "let's count again."

**1  2  3  4  5  6  7  8  9  10 !**

*Uno   dos   tres   cuatro   cinco   seis   siete   ocho   nueve   ¡diez!*

(oo-no) (doss) (trayce) (kwa-tro) (theen-co) (sayss) (see-et-ay) (o-cho) (nu-eb-ay) (dee-eth)

**11        12        13        14        15**

*once      doce      trece     catorce    quince*

(on-thay) (doe-thay) (tray-thay) (kat-tor-thay) (keen-thay)

**16              17              18              19              20 !**

*dieciséis      diecisiete      dieciocho      diecinueve      ¡veinte!*

(dee-eth-ee-sayce) (dee-eth-ee-see-et-ay) (dee-eth-ee-o-cho) (dee-eth-ee-nueb-bay) (bayn-tay)

Moucheboeuf counts:

**1   2   3   4   5   6   7   8   9   10 !**

**11  12  13  14  15  16  17  18  19  20  !**

38

"It's that one," cries Granville, "everyone *mira,* look – balloons! Let's knock *a la puerta (a la pwer-ta)*. Now remember, when you are invited to someone's *casa,* you have to be on your best behaviour, otherwise you will not be invited back if you're *tonto.*"

B. A. Lee

"That's right", adds Moucheboeuf, "and when you are told it's time to leave, it's time to leave. No tantrums. You just say, 'thank you for inviting me'. Let's knock."

*Toc, toc, toc, (toc) a la puerta,* knock, knock, knock on the door.

The door opens and someone says: "*¡Entra! (en-tra)* Come in everybody!"

It's Mooey Vaca. All the *ositos* say, "*Es mi amiga (am-ee-ga)*. She's my friend."

They go in and Mooey Vaca greets them by saying, "*¡Bienvenidos!* *(bee-en-ben-ee-dos)* Welcome! *Hola* Granville, *hola* Moucheboeuf.

*Buenas tardes* *(bway-nass tar-dace)* Trixie, good afternoon to you as well Jolie Holly."

Mooey Vaca asks how her friends are:

**(CHANT!)**

"*¿Cómo estáis (ess-tice), cómo estáis, cómo estáis?*
How are you?
*¿Cómo estáis, cómo estáis, cómo estáis?*
How are you?"

All reply:
**(CHANT!)**

"*Muy bien gracias, muy bien gracias, muy bien gracias,*
Very well thank you.
*Muy bien gracias, muy bien gracias, muy bien gracias,*
Very well thank you.

*¿Y tú?*" *(ee too)*

"*¡Bien!* I'm fine, thank you!" responds Mooey Vaca. "*¡Mira!* Everyone, a bouncy *castillo!* And you're just in time for the party games. The first *juego* is *escondite* *(esk-on-dee-tay)* out in the garden."

"*Me encanta* *(may en-can-ta)* hide and seek," says Granville.

40

"I love it also", Moucheboeuf agrees.

"Then we're playing *juego de las sillas*" *(kway-go day las seel-yass )*, adds Mooey Vaca.

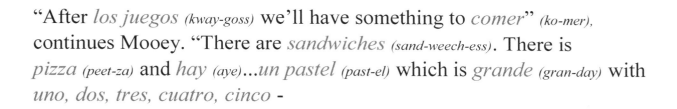

"*Me gusta (may gooss-ta) el juego* musical chairs", states Jolie Holly.

"I like it too", says Trixie.

"After *los juegos (kway-goss)* we'll have something to *comer*" *(ko-mer)*, continues Mooey. "There are *sandwiches (sand-weech-ess)*. There is *pizza (peet-za)* and *hay (aye)...un pastel (past-el)* which is *grande (gran-day)* with *uno, dos, tres, cuatro, cinco* -

**1   2   3   4   5**   candles on it. Also daddy is doing a barbecue.

Come and see who else is *aquí. Hay,* Cheesy Quackers and Crispy *Pato.*" *(pa-toe)*

The *ositos* sing:

**(CHANT!)**
"Cheesy Quackers, Cheesy Quackers, *y su (ee sue) amigo* - Crispy! Cheesy Quackers, Cheesy Quackers, *y su amigo* - Crispy!"

Who else is there?

*Cachorro El Perro (kat-chor-ro el per-ro), Cachorro El Perro*
Puppy The Dog, Puppy The Dog,
*Cachorro El Perro, Cachorro El Perro,*
Puppy The Dog, Puppy The Dog -
along with Mini Vaca, Mooey's little cousin.

Bunny *Conejo (kon-ay-kho)* the rabbit, *Chimichanga (chim-ee-chan-ga)* the Kanga
and the two monkeys – brothers Sami and Scruffy *Mono (mon-o)*, are there
as well. Also, Minty *Oveja, (obay-ka)*, the sheep with little Babby Lamb
Kebabby and the frog called -

*Boca Loca Lengua Larga (bo-ka lo-ka leng-wa lar-ga)* Crazy Mouth Long Tongue,
*Boca Loca Lengua Larga* Crazy Mouth Long Tongue.

Everyone says *hola.*

Then Mooey Vaca's *mamá (mam-a)* introduces herself to the *ositos.*

"*Me llamo (may lya-mo) señora (sen-yor-a)* Vaca."

Then she asks Granville what his name is:

**(To the tune of: Skip To My Lou, My Darling)**
"*¿Cómo te llamas? (ko-mo tay lya-mass) ¿Cómo te llamas tú?*
*¿Cómo te llamas? ¿Cómo te llamas tú?*
*¿Cómo te llamas? ¿Cómo te llamas tú?*
What is your name?"

Granville replies: "*Me llamo, me llamo* Granville, *se llama (say lya-ma), se llama* Moucheboeuf, *somos, somos ositos* - we are teddy bears!"

She then asks Jolie Holly her name.

**(sing to the same tune)**
"*¿Cómo te llamas? (ko-mo tay lya-mass)*
*¿Cómo te llamas tú?*
*¿Cómo te llamas? ¿Cómo te llamas tú?*
*¿Cómo te llamas? ¿Cómo te llamas tú?*
What is your name?"

"*Me llamo* Jolie Holly, *se llama, se llama* Trixie, *somos, somos ositos* - we are teddy bears!"

"*¡Encantado!*" *(en-kant-ad-doe)*, booms a deep voice coming from behind the *ositos.* They all turn around. It's Mooey Vaca's *papá. (pap-pa)*

"*¡Pan tostado (tost-ad-oe) señor (sen-yor)* Vaca!", reply the Magic Bag *Ositos.*

"*¿Pan tostado?*", laughs Mooey's *papá.* "That means toast. You don't shake hands and say toast'! You say '*encantado*', pleased to meet you. Not *pan tostado!* Not toast!"

Mrs Vaca asks Moucheboeuf if he would like *una bebida (oo-na beb-ee-da).*

43

Moucheboeuf replies:

**(To the tune of: Day O/Banana Boat Song)**
"*Q-u-i-e-r-o, q-u-i-e-r-o, (key-ero)*
*Quiero zumo de naranja por favor. (key-ero thoo-mo day nar-an-kha  por fab-or)*
*Q-u-i-e-r-o, q-u-i-e-r-o,*
*Quiero zumo de naranja por favor.*
I'd like, oh I'd like,
Orange juice, p-l-e-a-s-e."

*Las chicas* ask for *limonada (lee-mon-ad-da)* and Granville asks for,

**(CHANT!)**
"*Agua, agua, (ag-wa)*
Water, water, water,
*Agua, agua,*
Water, water, water,
*Agua, agua,*
Water, water, water,
*Agua, agua,*
Water, water, water - *¡por favor!*"

*La señora* Vaca fetches the drinks. As Granville is drinking his *bebida,* he gulps and cries out, "There was a *pez (payth)* in my *bebida!*"

"A *pez* in your *bebida?* A fish in your drink?", they all exclaim.

"*Sí.* Yes! A fish in my *bebida!* I've just swallowed it!", says Granville.

"That was like the little *pez espada* *(payth esp-ad-da)*
in *mi limonada* that ate my *tostada* *(tost-ad-a)*
*y* *(ee)* *mermelada!*" claims Cheesy Quackers.
"I was having *desayuno esta* *(ess-ta)*
*mañana,* when the little *pez espada,*
the swordfish, in my *limonada,*
jumped out of the *limonada,*
took my *tostada,* which I'd spread
with *mermelada,* then the little
*pez espada* from the *limonada,* leapt
back in to the *limonada* and ate my
*tostada* that was covered in *mermelada.*"

"Eh?", says everyone confused. "Are you crackers, Cheesy Quackers?"

Now, Moucheboeuf has hold of the present. He sings:

**(To the tune of: The Wheels On The Bus)**
"*Tengo un regalo*
*¿Qué, qué es? ¿Qué, qué es? ¿Qué, qué es?*
*Tengo un regalo*
*¿Qué, qué es?* What is it?
I've got a present
What is it? What is it? What is it?
I've got a present
*¿Qué, qué es?* What is it?"

"Let me *adivinar*", says Mooey Vaca, "it's some
*caramelos. (karra-mel-loss) ¡Me gustan los caramelos!*
*¡Me gu-u-u-u-u-stan los caramelos!*
*¡Me gu-u-u-u-u-u-u-u-ustan los caramelos!*"

Everyone shouts: "We all like sweets!"

**(To the tune of: The Mexican Folk Song - La Bamba)**
"*Caramelos, caramelos,*
*Caramelos, caramelos,*
*Me me me gustan,*
*Me me me gustan,*
I like sweeties, I like sweeties."

"It's not sweeties", says Moucheboeuf.

"Oh! Not *caramelos!* Well then, *es un juguete.* A toy", guesses
Mooey. "*¿No?* It's a *libro* - a book. *¿No? Es un juego, ¿verdad?* (ber-da)
*¿Verdad no?* Isn't it?"

46

**(CHANT!)**
"*¡Sí, sí, sí -*
*sí, sí, sí -*
*sí, sí, sí, sí, sí,* yes, yes, yes!

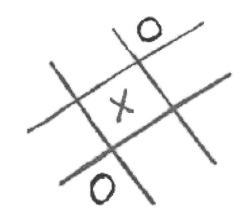

It's Tic-tac-toe", came the reply from
the Magic Bag *Ositos.*

"Tic-tac-toe? *¡Maravilloso! (marra-beel-yo-so)* Marvellous!
*Muchas (moo-chass) gracias* everyone", says a grateful Mooey.
"*¡Me gusta mucho (may goo-sta moo-cho) el juego* Tic-tac-toe!"

"Now", booms Mr Vaca "when you go into *el jardín* you will see a
barbecue but make sure you DON'T go near the barbecue because it is
*CALIENTE! (kal-ee-en-tay) ¡CALIENTE!* HOT! *¡MUY, MUY CALIENTE!*
VERY, VERY HOT! *La barbacoa (bar-ba-ko-a)* is made out of fire - and
what does fire do to you?"

"It burns you and hurts you!",
all the guests shout.

Mooey's *papá* continues,
"So, don't go near *la barbacoa*
and don't *¡TOCAR NADA!*
*(toe-kar na-da)*

DO NOT TOUCH ANYTHING!

**(CHANT!)**

*¡NO TOQUÉIS! ¡NO TOQUÉIS! ¡NO TOQUÉIS!* *(no toc-ace)*
DO NOT TOUCH! DO NOT TOUCH! DO NOT TOUCH!

**(CHANT!)**

*¡PELIGRO! ¡PELIGRO!* *(pel-ee-gro)*
DANGER, DANGER!
*¡PELIGRO! ¡PELIGRO!*
DANGER, DANGER! OK?"

"*¡De acuerdo!*", everyone responds, with thumbs raised.

"Also", Mr Vaca warns, "we've got a pond at the bottom of
*el jardín* with a *cocodrilo* *(kokoe-dree-loe)* in it and he'll bite your
*piernas* *(pee-ern-ass)* off if you go near the pond and then you won't be
able to bounce on the bouncy *castillo* without your legs, will you?
So, DON'T go near the pond! *De acuerdo?* OK? You NEVER go
near a pond by yourself in case you fall in, do you?"

48

"*¡PELIGRO! ¡PELIGRO!*
DANGER, DANGER!
*¡PELIGRO! ¡PELIGRO!*
DANGER, DANGER!"

"*¡De acuerdo!*", everyone agrees.

The Magic Bag *Ositos* really enjoy
*la fiesta.* First, they play *escondite* and
musical chairs, then they all wait their turn
to go on the bouncy *castillo.* (Only a few
of Mooey's friends are allowed on at the
same time, you see, in case someone
bumps their *cabeza*).

*¡Salta! ¡Salta! Salta! ¡Salta! Salta! ¡Salta! (sal-ta)*
Jump! Jump! Jump!
*¡Salta! ¡Salta! ¡Salta! ¡Salta! ¡Salta! ¡Salta!*
Jump! Jump! Jump!

After the party games they sit down to eat. Then Mrs Vaca brings in the
birthday *pastel.* It looks yummy. There are 5 lit *velas (bay-lass)* on it –

# 1   2   3   4   5 -

*uno, dos, tres, cuatro, cinco*

and all Mooey's *amigos* and *familia* *(fam-eel-ya)* wish her *feliz cumpleaños.*
*(fel-eeth kump-lay-an-yose)*

Mooey, with a big puff, blows out the **1  2  3  4  5** *velas.*

Mooey's *mamá* cuts the cake into portions. She then picks up a
piece of *pastel* and is about to bite into it when everybody shouts:
"*¡Pastel* picking *mamá*, put that *pastel* down!"

"Our guests should have the first slices of *tarta* *(tar-ta)*", *el señor* Vaca
advises.

Later they are all having fun playing
'What's the time Mr Wolf?'
Mooey's *papá* is Mr Wolf.

"*¿Qué hora es, señor Lobo?*
*(kay ora es sen-yor lo-boe)* What's the
time Mr Wolf?", they all enquire.

"*Es la una,* it's one o'clock.
*Son las dos (sonn)*, it's two o'clock.
*Son las tres....¡Es hora de comer!*",
screams Mooey's dad as he chases after everyone.

"Oh that was really good fun. It was,
**(CHANT!)**
*Divertido, divertido, (dee-ber-tee-doe)* fun, fun, fun,
*Divertido, divertido,* fun, fun, fun.

But it's time for us to go home. Is it really 3 o'clock?", sighs Granville.

On leaving, they all say *gracias* and *adiós* (add-ee-yose) to Mooey and his *mamá y papá* and *hasta pronto* (ass-ta pron-toe) to all their *amigos*. No-one had been silly – nobody had touched the barbecue or went near it and so no-one had got burnt and ended up in *hospital* (osp-ee-tal) and no-one went by the pond and was bitten by the crocodile, although Cheesy Quackers had a narrow escape! Nobody had any tantrums when they were leaving either. In fact, everyone had been ever so good and so Mrs Vaca said the Magic Bag *Ositos* and Mooey's other *amigos* could come to tea another day.

51

"Come on Magic Bag *Ositos*", sighs a tired Granville, "time to go back to our cave in *la bolsa mágica.* Let's say thank you very much and goodbye."

All: "*¡Muchas gracias y adiós!*"

And off they go singing:

**(CHANT!)**
*"Somos somos ositos*
We are teddy bears
*Somos somos ositos*
We are teddy bears
*Somos somos ositos*
We are teddy bears
*Somos somos ositos*
We are teddy bears, hey!"

"*¡Hasta pronto!* See you soon!"

And that was - the story!

THE *FIN* *(feen)*

If you have enjoyed this book, you might like to look out for other books in the series...

Feel free to contact me if you wish to know about forthcoming books or if you have any questions.

**Website:** http://pdavie8.wixsite.com/author
**Email:** pdavie07@gmail.com

*Be sure to leave customer feedback on amazon – thank you very much!*

# ¡Hasta pronto!

Made in the USA
Columbia, SC
31 July 2018